The journey to greatness

Understanding and experiencing the principle of God with you.

Michael Andam
The journey to greatness

Understanding and experiencing the principle of God with you.

CreateSpace

Published by CreateSpace
IBSN 978-1-9998846-0-4

Cover design by Rachel Halili
Website: www.rachelhalili.com

To
Elianne, Micaiah and Danielle

Content.

Introduction

Throughout the generations, it has been Almighty God's plan and desire to be with His children. He demonstrated this when He created Adam and Eve. Although Adam and Eve did not wholly trust in God's word but rather chose to believe otherwise to become gods' thus falling victims to the devils trickery, God's original plan remained intact. He is always looking to be with us even though our continuous desire to sin separates us from Him. He always strives to get us back on track because of His enormous love for us.

"God with us": This short sentence makes all the difference. We should be aware that dreams are vital. If you have stopped dreaming, do start again.

There seem to be many doctrines circulating around the world concerning the prosperity of Almighty God's children. Many are teaching that the followers of Jesus Christ must never experience what is described as hardships or life challenges. Many followers have come to understand that with God as their Father they should never experience challenges. Some of the scriptures on God's blessing and the principles of giving have been 'fatally' distorted deceiving many Christians.

On the other hand, the lessons of life set up by God are learnt in challenging situations. It is in difficult situations and challenging times that we learn to build our character through exercising and increasing our faith, trust and resilience in Jesus Christ and His ability to fulfil His promise for us. Personally I know that the greatest lessons of my life were learnt during serious and unbelievable challenging times. I have learnt that I am able to minister far more effectively to many on life situation areas I have experienced. For example, I am able to truly comfort people in times of their loss of a father, child, sister and brother through painful experience and God's amazing comfort and healing.

There are serious life challenges that some of my fellow brothers and sisters are going through that are simply mind blowing. However, the word of God is still powerful and does not change. God is with us. He is working something greater for our lives. We are not to give up even if the pain and challenges seem to worsen. We are to understand that God is still in control and nothing takes Him by surprise. We should continue to look up to God even when things seem out of control. He allows everything to happen to us for a reason and mainly for that to help us grow in our faith.

We are able to understand God's operation with regards to challenges in life by looking at what James said in scripture,

> "My Brethren count it all joy when you fall into various trials, knowing that the testing of your faith produces patience. But let patience have its perfect work, that you may be perfect and complete, lacking nothing."-James 1:2-4.

James' point is simple in that we should never loose focus on the fact that God is still at work in our life to do something greater. It is good to 'slow down' at times and look back to understand what God is doing. This helps me to evaluate what has been happening and continue to trust God for bringing me that far. What I have realised is that we like to take charge and control situations and circumstances in our life. Sometimes the thing we hold on to for so long and have 'faith' in for whatever comfort it bring us unconsciously could become our 'god.' This could be relationships, our well-paid jobs, some networks and many others. However, our loving Father wants us to trust Him completely so He alone can complete in us what He has started. Success does not come in one day. It comes daily through normal routines, schedules and walking in God's direction and trusting Him completely.

• **Chapter One**

Building the platform towards greatness.

The Bloodline

For this study, I will first introduce the ancestral lines of the main character to be discussed, which is Joseph, the son of Jacob (Grandson of Abraham) in the Bible. It is vital to understand that God Almighty is in the centre of our lives and totally in control of His creation. He blesses all those who trust and have faith in Him and the opposite is true. God's blessing is a divine empowerment that enables us to prosper in all aspects of life. We do not work to earn it. He chooses to bless anyone He pleases.

The opposite is the curse that comes on those who reject Him and His word. The blessing here is not only in material acquisition that has become part of the current popular doctrine being circulated around by some teachers in the church. God's blessing on our life is that divine enablement that helps us to prosper in all that we do within His will for us. It does not eliminate challenges and trials as contained in some doctrines as mentioned before. It rather ushers us into various phases of life with its challenges, pain and sorrows. However, the blessing of God over our lives brings us through victoriously because God is part of this journey and a main player in leading us.

Abraham, the biblical character is the great grandfather of our case study Joseph. Many a time our blessings or curses may have originated from our ancestors. The good news is that a past curse can still be broken because of the completed work of Jesus Christ on the cross that we will discuss briefly in the coming chapters.

Living under God's blessing provides His favour upon all spheres of our lives. The wrong doctrine circulating around is that you cannot go through any challenges when God is with you. It is the opposite. We are allowed to go through series of trials, tests and challenges to perfect our faith. It is not to 'teach us a lesson' as God does not have any interest in doing that. His presence with us helps with the releasing of blessings and favour upon us. This enables us to go through and come out victorious in every challenge we face.

Transfer from the bloodline
According to biblical history, Abram (Abraham) and his father Terah were idol worshippers. However, God visited Abram in a dramatic and powerful manner to change the cause of his life and many as well. Abraham's positive response as an act of obedience to this good news resulted in God's blessings and presence on generations upon generations. From this historic account, the storyline of greatness did not start with Terah, Abraham's father. He may have continued to serve idols. However, God decided to choose Abraham proving that He can choose anybody considered as ordinary to start something extraordinary. Now here is the evidence of what took place:

"Now the Lord had said to Abram, "get out of your country, from your family and from your father's house, to a land that I will show you. I will make you a great nation, I will bless you and make your name great, and you shall be a blessing. I will bless those who bless you, and I will curse him who curses you, and in you all the families of the earth shall be blessed."-Genesis 12:1-3.

From these scripture verses, God called Abraham who was called Abram at the time, to leave his homeland, family and all that were close and familiar to him to a place He would show him. Basically, God called Him to leave his comfort zone into the unknown. God promised to make him a great nation in another land unknown to him. A Promise He fulfilled. It was astonishing to see how this promise of blessing passed on from Abraham unto other generation to come after him. The promise to be a nation passed on to his future son called Isaac and future descendants.

First, the blessings passed on from Abraham (after God changed his name) unto Isaac. Isaac also passed it on to his son Jacob. The part of the blessing regarding the nation happened in Jacob's time together with his children.

Starting with Abraham, God had a series of events prepared for each of his descendants in coming into the promises made. Some of the experiences were challenging and others were sheer unpleasant depending on which point we view it. However, in all of this we should not forget that God is the One in charge of this and all of His creation. He said:

"I am God, and there is none like me. I make known the end from the beginning, from ancient times, what is still to come."
-Isaiah 46: 9-10.

This is true for all humanity, as God knows our end from the beginning. He is the master architect who first draws His plan (end) and builds it out (beginning). He is the one who gave you His purpose for your life. Everyone has a unique purpose in such a way that no other person can fulfil it.

About each having a purpose, God made it clear to us when He called the prophet Jeremiah. He said, "Before I formed you in the womb I knew you, before you were born I set you apart: I appoint you as a prophet to the nations." -Jeremiah 1:5. This is to emphasise the fact that God knows everyone before birth and have given him or her His purpose in life. The most important point here is that this purpose is not to benefit the individual alone, but also others such as generations, nations, communities and even the whole world.

Going back on track, the initial demonstration of God's favour on Abraham's life was astonishing. His nephew, Lot, was captured in a battle involving four strong kings against five kings. When Abraham received the news he did something that could be done only when God is with you. The favour of God on his life enabled him to take them on and won! At the time Abraham was not a warrior and it was only with God's help that he was able to defeat them. (Story in Gen 14:15-16)

The promise to Abraham was a demonstration of God's creative power. Abraham and his wife were past childbearing age. He was ninety-nine years when God made a covenant with him to biologically multiply him exceedingly. The couple had a divine visitation for a special promise of the birth of a son in the following year. Sarah indeed laughed when the Lord promised she would bear a child at her old age. Lets face it; I believe we would have all laughed. It was humanly impossible for that to happen.

"Now Abraham and Sarah were old, well advanced in age; and Sarah has passed the age of childbearing. Therefore, she laughed within herself, saying, "After I have grown old, shall I have pleasure, my lord being old also? -Genesis 18:11-12

God confronted Sarah on her laughter and said, "Why did Sarah laugh, saying, 'shall I surely bear a child, since I am old?' "Is there anything too hard for the Lord? At the appointed time, I will return to you, according to the time of life and Sarah shall have a son."- Vs. 14

God honoured His promise and gave the couple a son, Isaac. After some years something that we may describe as ridiculous happened. God asked Abraham to kill and sacrifice his only miraculous son of promise. We would have attributed this to the voice of the devil! We may have cast out the devil's voice from our head and even fasted and prayed against it. We need to train ourselves through close relationship to know the voice of God. However, Abraham obeyed and God prevented him from killing his son. God said,

"Do not lay your hand on the lad, or do anything to him, for now I know that you fear God, since you have not withheld your son, your only son, from Me. –Genesis 22:12

Divine providence
God was so pleased with Abraham's faith action that He further blessed him abundantly:

"By Myself I have sworn, says the Lord, because you have done this thing, and have not withheld your son, your only son- blessing I will bless you, and multiplying I will multiply your descendants as the stars of the heaven and as the sand which is on the sea shore, and your descendants shall possess the gate of their enemies. In your seed all the nations of the earth shall be blessed, because you have obeyed My voice."- Genesis 22:16-18.

This was the ultimate divine blessing that had the power to permeate into all the families of the world deep into the future from Abraham's time. This was possible because of ones man's obedience to let go of his most precious son. Among the entire test Abraham faced, this was the only one that God confirmed his fear of Him. The level of the test determined the reward he received. This does not give anyone the unnecessary mandate to exploit the church in giving money they do not have in the name on what has become so popular called 'seed sowing.'

Abraham was one hundred years old when Isaac was born to him. God's favour on them brought them laughter. "And Sarah said, "God has made me laugh, and all who hear will laugh with me."- Genesis 21:6

The promise of God for Abraham and his entire descendants was evident in the life of Isaac his son. He also faced serious challenges. Although the blessing and promise was on him, his wife was initially barren just like his mother Sarah. "Now Isaac pleaded with the Lord for his wife, because she was barren, and the Lord granted his plea, and Rebekah his wife conceived."-Gen 25:21

The children born to Isaac and his wife Rebecca were described as 'two nations.' The older was Esau and the younger Jacob.

Favour overcomes famines

One of the fascinating events that happened to Isaac was during a famine season. "There was a famine in the land, besides the first famine that was in the days of Abraham. Isaac went to Abimelech king of the Philistines, in Gerar." God asked him to stay in the land He chooses for him. What God said to him was a total reiteration of what was said to his father.

" Dwell in the land, and I will be with you and bless you, for to you and your descendants I will give all these lands, and I will perform the oath which I swore to Abraham your father. And I will make your descendants multiply as the stars of heaven, I will give to our descendants all these lands, and in your seed all the nation of the earth shall be blessed, because Abraham obeyed My voice and kept My charge, My commandments, My statues, My law."-Gen 26:3-5

Isaac obeyed God and lived in the land of Gerar. It is amazing how the promise passed on to him from Abraham, "...in your seed all the nation of the earth shall be blessed..." and He linked this with Abraham's obedience. Now lets look at how the effect of God's promise, blessing and favour on his life was described:

"Then Isaac sowed in that land, and reaped in the same year a hundredfold and the Lord blessed him. The man began to prosper, and continued prospering until he became very prosperous. For he had possessions of flocks and possessions of herds and a great number of servants. So the philistines envied him." –Gen 26:12-14

He went through some challenges as the envious Philistines stopped all the wells his father dug. The king eventually asked Isaac to leave their country as he had become very mighty in comparison to them. Isaac moved away to another place and settled.

The Lord visited him in this place and said to him, "I am the God of your father Abraham, do not fear, for I will be with you, and I will bless you and multiply your descendants for My servant Abraham's sake."-Genesis 26:24.

As time went by king Abimelech visited him with his army commander and one of his friends. I believe Isaac may have been suspicious of the visit and said, "why have you come to me, since you hate me and have sent me away from you?" Their answer helps with understanding that God's blessing and favour can attract those who do not even love or like us to come and make peace with us.

"But they said, "We have certainly seen that the Lord is with you. So we said, let there now be an oath between us, between you and us, and let us make a covenant with you, that you will do us no harm...you are now the blessed of the Lord."-Gen 26:28-29

Isaac and his wife Rebecca had a set of twins, Esau the oldest and Jacob, the younger one. The primary promise should have passed on to the first twin, Esau. However, he sold this right to his younger brother. He once came from a hunting trip hungry and asked his brother for a bowl of soup. Jacob asked him to sell his birth right to him in exchange of a bowl of soup. Esau readily did this, passing the promise to Jacob. Jacob eventually received the promise from God through Isaac. What a cheap exchange! Exchanging temporal hunger for long-term total blessing package covering all parts of life is never a wise thing to do.

We should not behave like Esau by giving up our long-term purpose for a short-term gratification and satisfaction. Anyone who desire to get into the place of God's greatness need to learn how to sacrifice in many areas of life for the sake of the long term goal. In this case, missing a lunch or holding the hunger to prepare something to eat would have saved his total packaged blessings (birth right).

Jacob also faced serious challenges such as with his father–in–law's deception and cheating. His father-in-law changed his wages ten times through deception (Gen 31:7). He even gave him the wrong daughter, Leah, as his wife after working seven years for Rachel. He had to work another seven years for Rachel (Gen29).

After marriage, his beloved wife could not bear children while her rival sister had many. However, God remembered her by opening her womb. She gave birth to her first son, saying, "God has taken away my reproach." She called him Joseph and said, "The Lord shall add to me another son."-Gen 30:24.

Jacob had a divine visitation when a Man (God) wrestled with him until the break of day. Jacob will not let go until a blessing was pronounced on him. "I will not let You go unless You bless me!" As the wrestling waged on He said to him "what is your name?" He said "Jacob." And He said, "Your name shall no longer be called Jacob, but Israel, for you have struggled with God and with men, and have prevailed."-Gen 32:26-28.

God blessed Jacob. The Man in the scripture is later spoken of as God. "And He blessed him there. So Jacob called the name of the place Peniel: "For I have seen God face to face, and my life is preserved." (Gen 32:29b-30).

As Jacob moved from Padam Aram, God blessed him. He also changed his name to Israel, meaning the prince of God. His previous name meant a deceiver. God changed the cause of his future as the carrier of His blessing for the generations to come.

God renewed the Abrahamic covenant with him. He said to him:

"I am God Almighty. Be fruitful and multiply, a nation and a company of nations shall proceed from you, and kings shall come from your body. The land, which I gave Abraham and Isaac, I give to you, and your descendant after you I give this land."-Gen 35:11-12

Summary and Points to ponder
- Against popular teachings, the Biblical doctrine on blessing is God initiated.
- God pronounces blessings and His desire is to be with you.
- Blessing is not solely the acquisition of material things such as houses, cars and bank accounts but one of the results of it.
- Abraham did not 'sow a seed' before he was blessed. The current popular doctrine of 'sow a seed' by giving money to 'receive' God's blessing is not how God's blessing work.

- There were occasions that all three Patriarchs experienced fear, even though God's protection was eminent.
- It is the blessing and favour of God, which enables us to be prosperous in all that we do.
- Blessing does not exempt us from challenges in life. It rather ushers us in to them, and that enable us to exercise our faith to achieve the victorious results.
- There are some occurrences that could happen in various generation that may not necessarily be described as curses. We studied that all the wives of the three patriarchs (Sarah, Rebekah and Rachel) had the issue of barrenness. They prayed to God on their wives' behalf and God did work miracles in those situations.
- The blessed children of God are not exempt from the attacks of Satan. However, positive response to the word of God always guarantees victory that brings glory to God and Jesus Christ. Christ has already done all to achieve our victory.

■ **Chapter Two**

Greatness Journey-Encased in Dream

The dream

As mentioned in the opening chapter, the main case study for this project is on one of the sons of Jacob. His name is Joseph. His journey to greatness is unique and demonstrates the hand and power of God's promise and our faith in His ability to accomplish it.

Here is Joseph's profile. (At the time of his story in Genesis 37)
- Age: 17
- He was the eleventh son of his father, and first son to his mother.
- Job: Caring for the family flock with his brothers.
- He brought bad report against his brothers.
- He was loved more than the others by the dad who made him a coat of many colours, which had great significance.

Joseph's father Israel, ignored biblical pattern of marriage and took two wives (and their maids servants) to produce a mixed family of twelve sons. The tension in the house was obvious as Jacob publicly showed favouritism to his second wife Rebecca and her two sons, especially Joseph. We need to apply wisdom from God in parenting as well as blessed children of God. Isaac's poor parenting style fuelled the tension among his children, which was expected.

The result was relentless hatred from his brothers. I believe that is not too remote, as many families may have experienced this. It is a dangerous thing to love one child above the others and show that openly as well. Bringing bad report to the father made him a kind of 'spy' on his brothers too. These days the young ones will call that behaviour 'a snitch.'

My brother in law shared an experience during his time in secondary school in a boarding house. It was one I could relate to as I went to a boarding house as well. In boarding house the student are 'together' on one side and the staff on the other. That is the culture. However he said, one classmate decided to be a 'spy' by reporting other students' bad behaviour to staff members. Many planned to do him harm and he never had a good time in school both academically and physically.

Now back to Joseph's story. To add to this hatred, Joseph had a dream and its implication naturally infuriated his brothers even the more. He said to them, "Please hear this dream which I have dreamed: "There we were, binding sheaves in the field. Then behold, my sheaf arose and also stood upright, and indeed your sheaves stood all around and bowed down to my sheaf." (Genesis 37:7).

Lesson one: He may not have understood or tried to understand the current family feud and tension, which he was at the centre of it. We need to be sensitive to the people around us even when the vision is so great and eager to share. In Joseph's case the brothers saw that as arrogance because he was the favourite of their father. They did not see beyond that favouritism to see what God was building in their brother.

Lesson Two: We need to grow and become mature. We should never share our God given vision, dream, or purpose with just anybody. We can share it with people who are themselves focusing on theirs and can guide you even if we are still maturing. It is not everybody who will share with the joy of you having such a vision. Some may even interpret it wrongly and may even feel threatened by your vision/dream. I have personally had experience with this issue in many ways.

This was precisely what God intended for Joseph. It was not for him to dominate and rule his brothers with pride as thought by his siblings. They said to Joseph "do you intend to reign over us, will you actually rule us" (verse 8a). This is why I warned that we must know who to share our vision and dreams with. Although Joseph only told them of the dream, they interpreted it as though he intended to rule over them. In other words they may have thought he made it up. Joseph needed to be prepared to take the responsibility of leadership for the future and he was about to go for training.

Lesson Three: We must always learn from our first mistake and never repeat them. Maturity sometimes comes after first experience. Joseph did not recognise that and repeated the first mistake one more time. He had another dream in which God gave him more clarity into his future. Once again he told his brothers and father.

"Look, I have dreamed another dream. And this time sun, the moon and eleven stars bowed down to me." Gen 37:9.

When his father was told, he rebuked him saying, "What is this dream you have had? Will your mother and I and your eleven brothers actually come and bow down to the ground before you?" (Verse 10). Once again, it might have been the way Joseph narrated his dream that may have lacked sensitivity. It could also have been that at that young age he may not have understood spiritual things. How he was to learn that in a very short time afterwards! Nevertheless, at the same time the father kept that in mind, although his brothers hated him the more. They indeed envied him for such dreams.

God can show you the vision and purpose for your life in dreams just as He did for Joseph. This vision is not only to make you great but mainly for the benefit of others too as mentioned in the introduction. You become a steward or custodian of a divine destiny with the lives of many at stake. The emphasis here is not our recognition in society as some celebrity or upper class citizen. Unfortunately with such status, some few people tend to look down on others. It is for us to seek God's direction on this and how we can be used as vessels to fulfil His purpose in us. God calling us is always a duty call to service. It is always about service to others.

What dream has God given you or your children? Is it making you feel more important than you normally feel? God has given you this to make you conscious of Him and to be focused on Him. It is only God who can make that dream He gave you come to pass. We cannot start with God and at some point abandon His directions and go our own way.

Summary and Points to ponder
- It is God who gives you a dream, vision and purpose in life.
- The preparation for the purpose of the dream start after the dream is given. God desire that we become sensitive and mature in dealing with people around us to bring peace and unity.
- The vision will be made clearer as God sees fit with time, His time. He may not show you everything involved in it, but we should be grateful for it and be patient as well.
- It is clear that Joseph and all of us need to learn how to take responsibility for the task given us starting from the given vision.
- We should be wise in the choice of people we share our God given vision, purpose and goals.
- We should take our vision and also that of our children very serious.

▪ Chapter Three

God's Vision-Attracts Hatred

Purpose for dream and vision

God's primary purpose for giving you a vision and purpose for your life is to benefit you and mainly others. He may not show you what group of people that should benefit initially, however it will be revealed with His time. Satan will do all he can to kill this. By so doing, he needs to do his best to hinder it using distractions and if possible destroy your life too. If your life is totally destroyed, what use will that vision be? If he is not able to kill it using all his known tools/ agents, then he will try to distract and redirect your focus on things away from your purpose. The purpose of God for your life is structured to promote the kingdom of God. This is the reason the devil is not happy with it.

There are others in biblical history whose vision and purpose attracted the wrath of the devil. Apart from Adam and Eve who he influenced to disobey God and change their destiny for worse, he also went out and attempted to destroy others such as baby Moses. The storyline of our study had progressed many years and the people of Israel were now enslaved in ancient Egypt. God called Moses to be the future deliverer of His people. At his birth, the king of Egypt decreed that all baby boys born to the Hebrew families should be killed. Even though the reason sounded different, the influence was from the devil to prevent the 'baby deliverer' to grow and fulfil the purpose of honouring God.

The birth of Baby Jesus also attracted the same fate for young children under the age of two. The reigning king at the time of Jesus' birth was Herod. He enquired from the chief priest and scribes when the Messiah was to be born. That place was confirmed to him. This all happened when the wise men visited him with the information that they have seen the star of the newly born King of the Jews. Herod asked them to find the Baby King and afterwards return with information to him. He was afraid and felt threatened by a Baby King! The wise men were warned divinely not to report to Herod. Herod got to know about it and in his anger sentenced all two year olds and under to death. The devil will try to 'kill off' your God given vision, including the carrier to avoid his continuous defeat. God protected the newly born King Jesus and others. He can protect yours too.

Devil's influence on hatred
The devil incited Joseph's brothers to hate him to the point of planning his murder. They sat down and literally planed and conspired to kill him. This shows the deep effect of Joseph's dream on them. It created envy, selfishness and pride in them. Satan took advantage of this flawed character of his brothers and used it to his advantage to carry out his evil agenda to stop God's future plans for humanity that Joseph would be involved with.

They waited for the opportune time. The devil uses his methods to manipulate and dominate all those available for him to use to destroy God's people hoping to destroy the vision of God. The point is that they could have "killed" their hatred for him because of their father's favouritism. However, they did not do so thus escalating their hatred to the point of murder. Uncontrolled anger can lead to hatred and even result in murder.

One day Israel (Jacob) sent Joseph to see how his brothers were doing in the fields with the sheep. When they saw him afar off they plotted to kill him. What was the motive for this? **"Then we will see what will become of his dream." –Gen 37:20b.** That was the reason for their envy!!. It was the purpose and vision for his life to be a great person. They were envious of the fact that his dream portrayed that they will serve him. They may have seen themselves as more important or deserving than him.

Many a time, the attack on you is the attack on your God given assignment, purpose or dream. It is vital to be aware of this and act accordingly as Joseph learnt through maturity. Although the father loved Joseph more than the others, the level of hatred was comparably low. It was only after the discovery of his future purpose that the brother's hatred reached boiling point. To pre-plan his murder was not a joke.

God intervened because of what would happen to Joseph in the future. It was His plan and He would always protect it and you as well. He needed Joseph to be alive to fulfil that. God who gave him the vision to save many lives in the future had to intervene. God will always protect His children and also the divine deposit in us by way of vision, purpose and His favour.

Rueben, one of the senior brothers tried to save Joseph. He suggested that they put him in a dry pit rather than killing him. His secret plan was to rescue him and bring him back home. However, during his absence the other brothers sold him as a slave without his knowledge. They sold him for twenty shekels of silver!

Process of hatred and its "explosion"

Result of envy: Joseph's brothers just could not stand the sight of him. They saw him afar off and plotted to murder him to end his dream. Joseph was not under the protection of his loving father at this time. It was their opportunity to 'end it all.'

Hatred is a product or fruit of selfishness. Was Rueben truly interested to help Joseph? As the first-born, Rueben had committed a grievous sin previously against his father by sleeping with his concubine Bilhah. (Gen 35:22b). He may have tried to restore some peace with his father by his desire to rescue Joseph and bringing him back to the father. These were the steps they took to complete their plan of hatred to kill Joseph:

- They stripped Joseph of his coat of significance. Afterwards they put him into the dry pit as suggested by Rueben.
- After putting him in the pit, they sat down to eat a meal. They still had appetite to eat! What a cold hearted bunch!

After having their meal they saw a company of Ishmaelite on their way to Egypt. Judah, one of the brothers convinced his brothers not to kill Joseph but rather sell him to the Ishmaelite. The brothers listened and agreed to do that. "...so the brothers pulled Joseph up and lifted him out of the pit, and sold him to the Ismaelites for twenty shekels of silver. And they took Joseph to Egypt."-Genesis 37:28.

Let us review Joseph's path to greatness so far from his point of view.

- He was loved by his father and hated by his brothers.
- He had two dreams that meant he would rule over his family one day.
- He went to check on his brother's welfare and was sold as a slave to some strangers.

Putting yourselves in Joseph's place, how will you feel at this moment in time? You have such a great dream and future but now all seem to be lost. We may have been tempted to ask the same old questions, "where is God when I need Him most." "Why didn't God do something to prevent this from happening to me." "Did He actually give me this dream or my brothers were right in saying I made it up?" Have you been there before? I have!

In all this, Joseph did not doubt his God or his dream. This is the attitude we need to demonstrate. In the face of extreme attack on God's word for us, we need to protect that word, as it will continue to uphold us. It will give us hope, which the Bible describes as an anchor to hold us steady as we sail through the rough paths of life. We should remember that God is with us.

Summary and Points to ponder on

- The people who are supposed to love you may do the opposite for whatever reason. This is usually something we may not be able to help or influence.
- Those close to you can betray and reject you. They may continue to lead their normal life after 'destroying' yours either deliberately or not deliberately.

- In all things we must continue to trust in God especially when the going gets tougher and life seems unbearable.
- Joseph may not have thought that would happen to him, but it did.
- God's timing is vital and we must understand that He is always on the look out for you.
- It doesn't matter what people plot against you, it is God's presence with you that matter most.

$$\boxed{\quad\blacksquare\quad \textbf{Chapter Four}\quad}$$

Vision Under Attack?

Sold into slavery: overcoming hatred/temptation and rejection.
After the brothers sold Joseph as a slave to some strangers, he was taken to a place far away from home. Joseph is now away from his 'comfort' zone, familiar people and environment, his family especially his beloved father and little brother Benjamin. This sounds familiar to what happened to his great grandfather Abraham when God called him and blessed him. The difference is that Abraham did not experience life as a slave.

"Meanwhile the Midianites sold Joseph in Egypt to Potiphar, one of Pharaoh's officials." –Genesis 37:36.

Potiphar's likely profile:
He was the captain of the King's guard. It has been suggested that he was in charge of the police and could have been the chief executioner. His duties involved destroying those who offended the rulership without trial.
He was a wealthy official with material possessions and servants to attend to him.
He had enough resources to buy Joseph to add to his servant base.

Initially I believe Joseph was seen as one of the slaves in the house of Potiphar. Joseph would have definitely experienced the culture shock, possibly language barrier, and a total different environment. He was no longer under the godly leadership of his father but rather in a heathen environment.

Potiphar, Joseph's new master noticed that God Almighty was with this young slave. It must have been obvious for Potiphar to see the tremendous difference in his wealth when

Joseph came into his household. There must have been a clear difference between what Almighty God was doing in his family through Joseph compared to that of his Egyptian idols!

"The Lord was with Joseph and he was a successful man." –Gen 39:2.

God's favour- Divine promotion

God's favour also comes with divine promotion in order to aid towards the preparation for executing other parts of the vision. Potiphar puts Joseph in charge of his entire household as he found favour in his eyes. The result was that God blessed everything Potiphar had both in the house and in the field. What a God!! All happened because of Joseph's presence in the house. He had God with him, which made all the difference. We should never underestimate the presence of God with us in any situation. Whether we are studying at school or working, our presence carries a special favour from God that has the ability to prosper all that we do.

The favour of God on Joseph would have been so powerful enough for Potiphar to leave all he had in the care of a foreign young slave. "Thus he left all that he had in Joseph's hand, and he did not know what he had except for the bread he ate."-Gen 39:6a. This was unusual, as slaves did not have this privilege. When you are ushered into an esteemed privilege because you love God, you need to acknowledge Him.

It may seem normal for us to read and think that all went well for Joseph at the end. The same cannot be said about us because our story is still being written. We are privilege to have his complete story in the Bible. We should remember that he did not have the Bible as we do to see the end of his suffering and the beginning of an unprecedented greatness. His life was part of the development of the Bible teaching for us.

It is interesting to know that God always show you part of the dream, which arouses our motivation to focus and take action towards it. He will not show you the entire path leading to it. I believe that may discourage us. I am experiencing this too.

In all this, Joseph did not complain and blamed it on his brothers or even on God. He maintained his trust and faith in God Almighty. This could be what we would normally be our reaction when we are confronted with various life challenges: "It is because of my background that this is happening." "It is because of such and such..." "God brought me this far to leave me because..." "This is so because I live in this country..."

In the face of life challenges, your godly values will keep you from falling into danger. It will steer you clear of all evil attractions that lead to the damnation of the soul. Here is one great way the Bible describes it:

"Delight yourself also in the Lord, and He shall give you the desires of your heart. Commit your way to the Lord, trust also in Him, and He shall bring it to pass. He shall bring forth your righteousness as the light, and your justice as the noonday."- Psalm 37:4-6

How can a slave prosper? This cannot be measured against current popular materialistic doctrines, as he had no material wealth as a slave. It also challenges the popular non-biblical teachings on prosperity floating around of late. It is not the acquisition of only physical things that defines one's prosperity, but God with us. This means God's blessing on our life does not depend on the material things we have. He blesses us so much so that all that we do and touch results in blessings, increase and with peace. The outcome of God's blessing and prosperity could also involve spiritual, academic, wisdom, health and material things.

Summary: Points to ponder on.
- You can be a 'slave' but not enslaved. Joseph did not allow himself to be enslaved by the circumstance.
- Your dream cannot be enslaved in anyway as it comes from God.
- We do not return hatred for those who hate us. Joseph did not resent his brothers even for what they did to him.

- The most important thing in life is to have God with you and nothing else. All the others will fall in place with God leading you step by step.
- You may not qualify for something great, but God with you could usher you into greatness that will amaze you. Joseph had authority over all that Potiphar had. It does not happen to slaves.
- God's favour on your life will open unusual doors for you even in strange environments.
- Your status in life including education has nothing to do with what God desires to do in your life. We must not allow anyone to deceive us to do something in order to receive from God in this aspect.

Chapter Five

God With you: Overcoming Temptation.

(Genesis 39)
Along the path to greatness are many trials, temptations and tests, which we have seen Joseph gone through sections of it. As life was improving and maybe becoming a bit bearable and quite comfortable, something unpleasant happened to Joseph once again. His blessing also came with the physical looks!! "Now Joseph was well-built and handsome" –Gen 39:6b

Long-term success over short-term sin
After some time Potiphar's wife 'noticed' these features on Joseph. "And it came to pass after these things his master's wife cast longing eyes on Joseph, and she said, "Lie with me."-Verse 7.

Many may have wondered about this action of a married woman of the calibre of Potiphar's wife. It may have been an abomination to many to commit adultery. However, some women do not see anything wrong with having multiple partners, extramarital affairs or pre-marital sex. These are now accepted as norm in some societies including the western world these days anyway.

Moral values and convictions
Joseph was able to refuse this offer that many may have embraced at his age. This was Joseph's response: "My master does not concern himself with anything in the house; everything he owns he has entrusted to my care. No one is greater in this house than I am. My master has withheld nothing from me except you, because you are his wife" (verse 9a)

This was Joseph's moral reason for refusing her evil offer. Likewise this is what we all need to do when confronted to chose pleasure over godly values and morality; **"How then could I do such a wicked thing and sin against God."** This was his main reason for not succumbing to this woman's constant persistence on sleeping with her. Joseph did not lose his fear of God even in an idol-infested land. He had all the opportunity to do it but refused because of his fear of God.

Joseph did not want to jeopardise his relationship with God by committing the sin of adultery. He may have understood the consequence and pain of negative actions and it's effect on others. Joseph was thinking about the future and would not destroy it with a temporal gratification of sin. Joseph's strategy was to avoid the lure of sin together with its opportunities that came with it together with its frustration and negative outcomes.

Although the temptation went on and on, Joseph refused even to be alone with her. Joseph had gone to execute his task in the house on one occasion. The men in the house were not inside. Potiphar's wife ceased the opportunity to lure Joseph once again. She literally grabbed hold of his garment and said "come to bed with me." (Verse 11-12). Joseph had already put his strategy together which is never to sin against God. What was his action on this occasion? "But he left his garment in her and, and fled and ran outside." Gen 39:12.

False Evidence at hand
Potiphar's wife action:
After Joseph run out of the house she had in her possession his garment as evidence. She planned her deceit and carried it out as follows:

She called to the men of the house and narrated her 'cooked lies.' "See, he has brought in to us a Hebrew to mock us. He came in to me to lie with me, and I cried out with a loud voice. And it happened, when he heard that I lifted my voice and cried out, that he left his garment with me, and fled and went outside." Gen

39:14-15. That was her story well rehearsed to the men to rally some kind of support for her.

The woman kept the garment until the husband came home. She 'played back' her rehearsed lies claiming Joseph, the slave tried to rape her. She had the 'evidence' in her hand to show the husband, which have been snatched from Joseph and used as false evidence. It is better to be falsely accused than to sin and face punishment. God will always vindicate us when we are wrongly or falsely accused because of our love for him.

The result

Potiphar was so enraged that he put Joseph in prison where the king's prisoners were kept. If Potiphar was the chief executioner, he could have engineered for him to be killed. The penalty for rape at the time was death. It could be possible that Potiphar did not believe his wife. Joseph's character and conduct in his house may have convinced him that he would not commit such a crime. However, the greatest Judge was with him and justice prevailed. Some may argue on the basis of him going to prison? God was still training Joseph on servant-leadership principles and had a great plan for him although it may have seemed everything was going downhill!!

In the sight of God he overcame temptation. Our response to temptation is crucial. We need to be determined not to destroy our relationship with our Father and also taint our future when put in a place of greatness or even in authority.

" No temptation that has overcome you except such as is common to man, but God is faithful, who will not allow you to be tempted beyond what you are able, but with the temptation will also make the way of escape, that you may be able to bear it"- 1Cor 19:13

We should see temptations as tests and one that we must pass. There is no temptation engineered to be extremely tougher than we can bear. We can overcome all temptation with the word of God spoken to us. When we see Satan's attempt for us to sin as tests to promote and make us strong, the fear of God and His word in us will cause us to triumph.

It will be appropriate to end this chapter with an example of overcoming temptation from Jesus Christ our saviour. Jesus went through the procedure of temptation and showed us the right way to overcome it. This gives us an example of how we can live a life as overcomers as well:

Jesus' example

After fasting for forty days and night, the Holy Spirit led Jesus Christ into the wilderness to be tempted by the devil. (Ref Matt 4:1). Jesus was now hungry after the fast. The devil's temptation was directed at what seemed to be the 'weakness' at that particular moment. "He said if you are the Son of God, command that these stones become bread." (Matt 4:3) Jesus' answer is simple but deadly to the devil, "it is written, Man shall not live by bread alone, but by every word that proceeds from the mouth of God." (Verse 4). Two more temptations followed and Jesus used the word of God to see him off.

First of all, we notice how the Holy Spirit led Jesus Christ to be tempted. Temptation is not a punishment from God but rather He allows us to be tested. Secondly it is only the devil that tempts us with the aim of getting us to sin against our heavenly Father. His main interest is to destroy our relationship with God. The weapon against falling into the devil's trap during temptation is to stand and act on the word of God. We overcome temptation by the word of God. The way of escape from temptation is using and acting on the word. In joseph's case running away from the physical temptation was just right.

Summary and points to ponder.
- Joseph did not forget his godly values, ethics and principles, which shaped his life. He feared God so much that he eschewed evil and sin. This was why he brought

bad reports concerning the characters of his older brothers previously.

- Although he did not have his father's godly guidance, he kept what he knew about God in his heart and demonstrated it. That 'seed' grew.
- Joseph knew that although he was no longer under the protection and comfort of his beloved father Jacob, he quickly realised that God his Father in heaven was always present with him. That was a great assurance, hope and comfort to him. Even in a foreign land full of idols, Joseph continued to fear God and worshipped Him alone without fear.
- We do not sin when we are tempted. On the other hand, falling prey to the temptation to fulfil its lust causes us to sin.
- In every situation God is still with you even when you do not think He is.
- The fear of God helps us to overcome any form of temptation. We need to always consider the long-term consequence of every action we take. There is always a reaction to every action taken as seen in the life of Joseph.

■ **Chapter Six**

Dreams under lock?

Solitary for divine discoveries

Our study from the last chapter concluded with Joseph been thrown into the king's prison for alleged 'rape' charge. God did not abandon him. He was still with him. There is something about God that may come as a surprise to many. He sympathises with us when we are treated unjustly, badly and especially rejected.

On the first day of his prison life, I believe Joseph did what many of us would normally do when we face a major change in life. He may have pondered or reflected on his life till date:

- Joseph was enjoying life as a young man with his family. He was unmistakably loved above all the children. He hated wrongdoing and reported his brothers' bad behaviour to his dad.
- His brothers hated him so much so that they caused him unbearable pain. They stripped him of his coat of significance and put him in a pit, contemplating on killing him.
- He was sold into slavery and later brought into a foreign land.
- God's favour made life a little bearable in the house of Potiphar as he learnt leadership skills without knowing about it. He learnt how to be responsible and accountable. His integrity was outstanding. God was with him.
- He is now suffering because of his fear of God to sin against both God and his master Potiphar. He is in jail

because he did what was right before God and upheld integrity and morality.

- Joseph had to readjust his life as a prisoner after having the freedom as a slave in the house of Potiphar.

Life in prison: Was God with Joseph in prison? "But the Lord was with Joseph and showed him mercy, and he gave him favour in the sight of the keeper of the prison."-Gen 39:21. That was the evidence that God did not leave him to fend for himself in prison. It was part of his journey.

Leadership skills identified (Genesis 39)

With God's mercy and favour, His face once again shone on Joseph to be identified immediately. The keeper of the prisons put Joseph in charge of all the other prisoners. The keeper had confidence in joseph so much so that he did not look into anything under his authority. We have to understand that this was not a normal thing even during that time. Here was the reason, "because the Lord was with him, and whatever he did, the Lord made it prosper." Gen 39:23b. The evidence was once again so clear that even these idol worshippers wanted to be part of his life. It did not matter to them that he was 'different,' both as a prisoner and foreigner. That is what 'God with us' can achieve.

God knew that the royal officials would be in prison at a certain time. He knows how to execute His plan for our lives at every stage. We also need to understand that God knows our end from the beginning. (Ref Isaiah 46:10) "Declaring the end from the beginning."

In view of this, he allowed specific trial or temptation or both to come Joseph's way to get him to meet these officials. It may sound very unusual even crazy and not something to look forward to. That is one of the reasons God does not necessarily show us everything on the path of our journey to greatness. Majority of His plan will not make 'human' sense to us.

Two officials of the kingdom offended the king of Egypt. (Gen 40:1-2). One was the butler and the other the Baker. In his anger the king imprisons both in the prison were Joseph was confined. The guard put Joseph with the two officials and his duty was to serve them. What happens afterwards proves that nothing happens in our life by chance. God orders our steps when we focus on Him. The apostle Paul puts it in this way, "And we know that all things works together for good to those who love God, who are called according to His purpose" (Romans 8:28). From our study Joseph fit perfectly into this description.

The king's butler and baker had a dream one night at the same time after spending some time in prison. (Gen40: 5). Joseph came to them the next morning and saw their dejection. He asked them what was making them so sad. They were sad because they thought there was no one to interpret their dreams. The officers of Pharaoh understood the importance and significance of dreams.

Identification of new gifts.
During our journey to greatness, God sets up opportunities to discover various gifts and talents He has given us, which would be needed in future. This continued with Joseph's journey as well:
The imprisoned royal officials told Joseph their dreams. Joseph is now familiar with his gift and knowledge about dreams. Once again Joseph saw the opportunity to introduce God Almighty into the situation in the same way he did with Potiphar's wife. Joseph said to them **"do not interpretations belong to God?** Gen 40:8b. They told him their dreams and with the power of God showed them the meanings.

Dream one: The butler saw a vine with three branches, which blossomed and produced grapes. He saw Pharaoh's cup in his hand.

Interpretation: Joseph said that in three day he would be restored back to his position as royal butler.
When the baker saw the interpretation of the butlers dream was good, it encouraged him to tell his.

Dream two: He saw that there were all kinds of baked goods in the top basket for Pharaoh. The birds came to eat of it on his head.

Interpretation: Joseph said in three days Pharaoh would lift off his head and hand him on a tree. The birds will eat of his flesh.

We should remember that Joseph never used to interpret dreams. The last time we associated him with a dream was when he had two that ended him where he is so far in our study. When you walk closer and closer with God and Jesus, He continues to unfold and reveal to you more and more of Himself and the gifts and talents needed to fulfil your given assignment.

After telling the butler what will happen to them Joseph asked him for one favour. This was because he was going to be restored by the king in three days. Joseph took the opportunity to ask for that favour. " But when all goes well with you, **remember me** and show me kindness; mention me to Pharaoh and get me out of this prison. For I was forcibly carried off from the land of the Hebrews, and even here I have done nothing to deserve being put in a dungeon" Gen 40:14-15.

The next three days was the celebration of the king's birthday. As expected the king made a feast for all his servants. The baker was to be killed and hanged exactly as Joseph said. However, the butler was restored but he did not remember joseph. "Yet the chief butler did not remember Joseph, but forgot him."-Gen 40:23.

Sometimes you will be forgotten by loved ones, people you look up to for help and motivation and many others. Do not perceive them as evil or wicked. The good news is that even though all may forget you **God never forgets you**. He is still working on you. God is your source of everything. Joseph was doing what everybody would have done. He was right in what he said. He did nothing wrong to deserve all the pain he went through all those years to date so far.

He was right in saying that he was forcefully sold into slavery and wrongfully accused of rape without being given the opportunity to defend himself. There was no justice or defence for a slave. He could have been put to death, but once again God preserved his life so he can fulfil his given destiny. Does that sound like you? Well it sounds like me for many years in similar situations!! In fact he was going through this path towards greatness because HE DID EVERYTHING RIGHTS!! It was not God's time for Joseph to come out of prison by the word of the butler at that moment.

Summary and points to ponder
- Your life challenges may seem to have worsened. However, it is God with you that will continue to give you favour and get you to the next higher level as His time go on.
- It is your dream from God that will take you to the next level.
- God will give us the needed gifts and talents to solve problems if that is needed to move us up His ladder and closer to our destiny of greatness.
- We need to continue to use our gifts and talents even when all seem lost and hopeless. It is through this that other gifts and talents unknown to us may come to the fore. Joseph discovered the interpretation of dreams at this stage.
- People you help in life may never remember or help you in any way especially when you needed that most. We should continue to love such people and rather trust God for His hand to continue to be in every circumstance we face. We need to wait for God's timing, which is always perfect.

Chapter Seven

God's purpose fulfilled

From prison to prime minister. (Genesis 41)
We should never seek or look up to people as our source of help. It was now two full years since the butler forgot all about Joseph in prison. The current review of his life may have included the betrayal from brothers who hated him, and now a friend who abandons him for a very long time. This is the reason we must only put our trust in the Lord Jesus Christ (God). Joseph did not become disillusioned or angry as his trust was in God.

It is now eleven years since he was sold to slavery and the interpretation of the official's dreams. His faith has been tested for eleven years. He had learnt a great deal of 'servant-leadership,' the type approved by God for His children. On the other hand, he had to wait for another two years as his friend, the king's butler forgot all about him.

Two full years pass and something interesting happened in the king's palace. It was to do with a dream one more time! Pharaoh had two dreams, which disturbed his sleep. (Gen 41: 2-7). He was troubled in his spirit when he woke up in the morning. He called for all his magicians and wise men, but none could interpret the dream for him. It is vital to know that the king of Egypt was so concerned about the dream that he sort for answers. This was a spiritual matter and he knew the significance of dreams.

How come his wise men could not help at this time? This dream had a divine purpose, which had nothing to do with Satan and his false powers being used by his magicians. God prepared this time to show His power and love for His son Joseph and for many people. There is a day and time when God will allow a situation where you alone are able to deal with it successfully with His help. It could be in any place, school, work, church and etc. It is to bring God glory.

I believe that the king might have been disappointed with his magicians and wise men's inability to help him. In that hopeless and tense situation, the chief cupbearer (butler) realised his mistake and said to Pharaoh, "Today I am reminded of my shortcomings, pharaoh was once angry and put me in custody in the house of the captain of the guard, both me and the baker." He continued to narrate to the king that Joseph interpreted their dreams. (Ref Gen 41: 9-13). He explained to the king that Joseph told them the meanings to their dreams, which turned out exactly as he said. The butler made mention of Joseph's origin as a Hebrew. "Now there was a young Hebrew man with us there, a servant of the captain of the guard." (Verse 12)-

God made sure the butler did not forget forever. Why? It was the right time on God's agenda for this to happen. As the creator of all things and Master of all situations, He caused this moment to take place. His name was about to be made great!

God's uplifting and glorification.
Pharaoh called for Joseph.
Could you imaging staying in the dungeon and not knowing what will happen to you each day? Remember he knew that the baker was executed from the same prison! To make things worse he was a foreigner. The man he told of his dream forgot him. Everything might have looked hopeless.

But God was still working hard and putting finishing touches to the whole journey. Remember God only take one second in a day to say to you: **" you have just crossed over the finishing line."** To Joseph this was when he was told; the king wants to see you. You cannot appear before the king in prison clothes.

"He was quickly brought out from the dungeon. When he had shaved and changed his clothes he came before pharaoh." (Verse 14)

One minute he was in the prison and the next here he was standing before one of the great leaders of the world at the time. He exchanged his prison clothes for cloth fitting for an audience with royalty.

Pharaoh said to Joseph: "I had a dream, and no one can interpret it. But I have heard it said of you that when you hear a dream you can interpret It." –vs. 15. This would have been a great opportunity to show off. But not with a man who give all glory to God. Joseph has learnt over the past decade how to please God in every situation. He had learnt how to conduct himself in the presence of officials such as Potiphar and the two officials who came into the prison. Before we study the outcome of what conversation went on between the King and Joseph, let us look at Pharaoh's initial words to Joseph. We read earlier how the butler introduced Joseph as a prisoner and a foreigner. However, notice that the king was not bothered about whether joseph was as a foreigner and prisoner or not. He was eager to have answers to his dreams. That is when God's time for your elevation comes.

The dream: In his dream he was standing at the bank of the Nile River when seven well-fed cows came out of the river and grazed in the meadow. Afterwards seven other poor, ugly and gaunt cows came up and ate up the first fat cows. According to the king he awoke from his sleep and later went back to sleep. He had a second dream whereby seven thin heads on one stalk devoured seven full and good heads on one stalk.

The king also informed Joseph of his magicians and wise men's inability to explain his dreams. I believe that God made it that way. They could have lie about the interpretation of it to the king. However, this was beyond their 'magical' and idol's power as a divine hand was in it. The dream came from God, hence their inability to explain as they were not his servants.

Joseph said to Pharaoh: Joseph gave Pharaoh the answer. Pharaoh's dream was interpreted as the coming of plenty of food for seven years and later famine in the land for another seven years. "The dream of Pharaoh are one, God has shown Pharaoh what He is about to do." verse 25. Joseph continued that the seven-year famine would be severe that no one would remember the previous years of plenty. "And the dream was repeated to Pharaoh twice because the thing is established by God, and God will shortly bring it to pass."-(Ref-Gen 41:25-32). In this fascination turn of event, Joseph pointed them to God and gave Him the glory. He continuously attributed the whole of Pharaoh's dreams to God.

Joseph's advice: On completing the explanation of the dream, he further gave advice on what was to be done to avert famine in the land. "And now let Pharaoh look for a discerning and wise man and put him in charge of the land of Egypt. Let Pharaoh appoint commissioners over the land to take a fifth of the harvest of Egypt during the seven years of abundance" (verse 33-34). In verses 35 – 36 Joseph continued to suggest his plan of action to the king. This was Joseph's strategic plan for the country concerning the officers he suggested to oversee the gathering of food in the plenty years:

"And let them gather all the food of those good years that are coming, and store up grain under the authority of Pharaoh, and let them keep food in the cities." (Verse 35)
"Then the food shall be as a reserve for the land for the seven years of famine which shall be in the land of Egypt, that the land may not perish during the famine." (Verse 36)

Question
Where did Joseph get all this business and political ideas? We knew him as a young shepherd. Like Jeremiah and others given in the Bible, God put into everyone gifts and talents, which we need not to 'study' in a classroom before knowing. This comes with your purpose during the journey. They come to the fore in specific times and situations especially when we have gone through some life experiences and learnt how to deal with those circumstances.

God takes time to develop our character and make sure that gift is used at the right time when needed to make a difference to our lives and that of many others. In Joseph's case, he learnt how to be sensitive and control the leadership potential deposited in him with the gifts as well over time.

The King's response to divine wisdom
After Joseph gave direction on what needed to be put in place, the plan seemed good to the king and his officials.

Pharaoh's response: "can we find anyone like this man in whom is the spirit of God? Then he said to Joseph "since God has made all this known to you, there is no one so discerning and wise as you."-Verse 38-39

God with you can create opportunities that you never dreamt of. This will be an opportunity for you to be heard and seen for His glory. It is a time God should be given the centre stage for the gift He has given you. That is exactly what Joseph did at any opportune time, giving God full glory and credit.

God's plan manifested
The divine promotion of Joseph was manifested in the physical. Pharaoh gave a speech on what should be done after putting Joseph in charge of affairs concerning the coming years of plenty and the famine to follow as given.

Pharaoh: "you (Joseph) shall be in charge of my palace, and all my people are to submit to your orders. Only respect to the throne will I be greater than you. I hereby put you in charge of the whole land of Egypt." Vs. 40-41
I believe that in reality Joseph's jaw may have literally dropped and thought to himself, "wake up from this unrealistic dream, you are still sitting in the prison dungeon."

Review: Notice that the king said Joseph would be in charge of his palace. The king's palace could be compared to modern day presidential palaces, which are normally regarded as the seat of power. Joseph is now appointed as the equivalent of a prime minister of Egypt!! He was going to be in charge of the seat of power in Egypt!! One minute he was in prison, a dungeon to be precise. Pharaoh made mention that Joseph is equal to him in ruling the nation. The only difference is that he is the King by the power of the throne. This is like the political system in the United Kingdom. Although the monarch is the head, it is the Prime Minister who carries out the operations of governing the nation.

Even in 'prison' we must realise that the purpose of God is never imprisoned. It will be fulfilled at God's own time after He has taken the time to prepare us to handle it. At first Joseph only saw his family bowing down to him. But now he has gone through enough training and experience learning how to be humble in the presence of God. He can now appreciate that the God who gave him the dream just fulfilled His purpose for him. His purpose as we just studied was different from what he saw in his dream. It is far greater than his dream. God is greater than any dream He gives us. We have just realised that God opened a greater door for Joseph to become a ruler in a foreign land even when he was a slave and a prisoner. This is how God works in our lives. His purpose is done first even before the part He shows us just as in Joseph's case.

Confirmation of change of state.
"Then Pharaoh took his signet ring from his finger and put it on Joseph's finger. He dressed him in fine linen and put a gold chain around his neck." Gen 41:42
The king was not just throwing words into space. He believed in what Joseph said because he recognised that it was the spirit of God Who was dwelling in him. It was the same Spirit of God that revealed what God was about to do. As the king, he had to honour his word.

From the scripture we read the king's action was a clear transfer of authority in the presence of all his officials. When God decide to lift you high for the benefit of others, He will do it in His own way. God does not need our permission to glorify His name in lifting us up unto greatness. All is done for His name to be glorified.

Public proclamation and affirmation.
"He made him ride in a chariot as his second-in-command and men shouted before him "make way" (or bow the knee). Thus Joseph was put in charge of the whole of Egypt." -Vs. 43. Joseph was thirty years when he entered into service as a prime minister. Afterwards, Pharaoh reassured Joseph that he has been given the great task of governing the land of Egypt. What he said to him would be his mandate to carry out the task given to him "I am Pharaoh, and without your consent no man may lift his hand or foot in all the land of Egypt." Vs.44

It took him thirteen years for all this to be fulfilled!!! The major lesson we can learn from this among others is that the timing for events to happen in our lives is so crucial. Most importantly this timing is on God's 'watch' and not ours. Our part is to wait and continue to have faith in this faithful God.

Summary and points to ponder
- God's dream for us is always hidden in His bigger and ultimate purpose for our life. Joseph's dream did not happen first. God's purpose did. Instead of eleven brothers and parents bowing down to him, God caused a whole nation to do so first. They did so first because Joseph attributed the solution to the future problem to God.
- God uplifts us mightily beyond our wildest dreams when we trust and glorify Him in all situations.
- It does not matter your gender, race, tribe or anything for that reason. We studied that Joseph who was a prisoner was made a prime minister because God was with him. Remember also that Pharaoh was made aware of the fact that this prisoner was a foreigner!! Never limit God in what He alone can do. Do not set limits on what He can do because of the things or circumstances you have either experienced or see around you.
- The situation that could destroy you becomes the building blocks for your journey to greatness when God is with you.

- The king of Egypt was convinced that his dream was very important and needed explanation. He did not care if a prisoner or a foreigner could do it. God can create a need where you will be the only one to have the solution. He is the One who 'makes' us into what He wants us to be.

■ **Chapter Eight**

Final phase of the journey. (Genesis 42-45)

Duties and responsibilities-service to humanity

The seven years of plenty came as Joseph predicted and his plan was put in place. The famine spread throughout the whole world according to Scriptures. This meant it affected Canaan, Joseph's homeland before he was sold into slavery.

Breaking news!!

Unfortunately there were no television or radio at the time to broadcast Joseph's promotion seven year ago that he was in charge of Egypt and their food distribution programme. All nations were coming to buy food from Joseph. He was the one all the officers reported to.

Eventually the severity of the famine was felt in Canaan. Joseph's brothers had to travel to Egypt to buy grain. They did not recognise Joseph as he was dressed as an Egyptian. On the other hand he did recognise them. The teaching is not on what he or they did, but rather how God fulfils dreams to the letter as intended.

Final Destination? Dream fulfilled?

Here are some of the important events and statements that fulfilled Joseph's dream.

"Now Joseph was the governor of the land, the one who sold grain to all its people. So when Joseph's brothers arrived, they bowed down to him with their faces to the ground." (42:7)

Well, they came and bowed down to Joseph as he said in the dream after about twenty-two years. Remember it was not the bowing down which was important, but the saving of the world from famine. God prepared him before time to preserve life. The dream about the moon and the sun was a worldwide influence and not just his family bowing to him.

One day during the visit of the brothers to buy food, Joseph could not control himself any longer as he had done previously. He was wearing Egyptian cloths and they did not recognise him as the brother they plotted to kill and later sold into slavery. He sent all his officials and servants out and afterwards made himself known to his brothers. He said to them "and now, do not be distressed and do not be angry with yourselves for selling me here, because it was to save lives that God sent me ahead of you." (45:5)

"But God sent me ahead of you to preserve for you a remnant on earth and to save your lives by a great deliverance." (45:7)

Joseph acknowledged the fact that all that happened was God's plan. God never wish or plan that we get hurt. But if that is the narrow road for us to get on to fulfil His dream to save and help others, then He will allow it. "So then it was not you who sent me here, but God" (45:8a)

Finally Joseph's father joined them in Egypt at his invitation. The dream is completed. Remember the mother died before Joseph was sold into slavery.

This applies to all of us. All good and perfect things come from ABOVE, from God alone. God gives us all good things that will also be needed by many as we have just studied in the story of Joseph. You may be called as an accountant, doctor, a pastor (all profession being equally good), however we all may face life challenges as Joseph did in various ways. It might not necessarily be exactly the same.

Joseph did well to represent God in an ungodly nation. We have a similar situation in the world. The western nations used to be under God Almighty. However, this has given way to secularism and the development of a pluralistic and multi-religious society. We as the ambassadors of Jesus Christ should do well to represent Him as well.

Joseph always made his identity known as a worshipper of God Almighty everywhere he went. We the followers of Christ must make Jesus known to people we come in contact with and the great difference only He can make in their lives.

Summary and points to ponder

- Your dream will surely come to pass as God intended.
- We should never hold grudges against those seen as causing our hurt and pain. They were involved because they may not have dedicated their lives to Jesus Christ to do the right things.
- As we face life's challenges and pain, we should hold on to our confident in the great plan of God for us. That is how we can overcome the hardship, pain and mistreatment that come with the challenges
- We should be proud to be part of the family of God. This does not come with us 'blowing the trumpet' of who we are. It must be seen in our daily life. It does not stop at times when things seem bearable. Joseph endured all situations and still made God known to the people always. He was an ambassador of God and was not afraid to demonstrate that.

■ **Chapter Nine**

Your gifts-For others benefit.

God's purpose first.

God's purpose was ultimately greater than the dream He gives us. Our dreams are embedded in God's purpose for us. Joseph's dream came second, after God saved humanity from dying of the grievous famine He knew was coming many years before Joseph was sold into slavery.

We should hold onto our dreams and at the same time be open enough to allow God to do His ultimate work in our lives. To be open here means we need to trust God and Jesus Christ daily in all situations that we find ourselves.

One of the vital things we can do is to use our gifts and talents in the face of extreme life challenges. This will be a challenge when your back is against the wall. How do you help others when you need help? Let us look at the possible outcome of a reverse of what would have happen to Joseph.

Overcoming Reverse and negative response

What would have happened if Joseph felt pity for himself, and decided not to help anyone, as he needed help too? Let us go back to what happened after the incident at Potiphar's house.

Joseph could have chosen not to demonstrate his leadership skills in managing people and places. He could also have decided not to use his God given gifts to help the Butler and the Baker. We all sometimes feel stretched when things are rough and do not feel like helping anyone. Everyone would sympathise with you, as you are experiencing challenges yourself. However, the God kind of life does not work like that. We are to help others even when we are facing our greatest life challenges.

In his anguish, Joseph had the heart to care for the welfare of other prisoners under his care. Joseph would have missed God's opportunity if he chose to ignore the sad countenance of the two royal prisoners. He would never have known their dream and missed God's new gift of interpretation of dreams for himself. He would never have asked the Butler to remember him when all went well with him. He would not have been to see Pharaoh the time he did.

The good news is that God always gives us second opportunities even if we miss the first. The important point here is not for us to miss the first when we are so close to Him.

Priority to help others
We should always remember who we are and carry on helping others to the best of our ability even when we are going through difficult times. My wife and I have faced various life challenges and had helped others in similar or worst state. These had ranged from financial to bereavements. One thing I realised is that in helping others; somehow our needs too are met. Do not bottle your gifts in times of challenges, let them out and see what other talents and gifts are hidden within you.

We should always remember that Godly greatness comes through difficult life challenges. No one has become great when living at ease with everything at his or her disposal. The great names in history such as Moses, King David, Jesus Christ and Nelson Mandela all faced impossible life situations. They rose above those challenges and made life better for many. It is our time to do the same like Joseph. Good practicing of our gifts and talents will make us better at demonstrating them as time goes on.

Summary and points to ponder
- God never forget what He says He will do. His ways are totally different from ours. That makes Him God and who

we are. He says, "For My thought's are not your thoughts, nor are your ways My ways, says the Lord. For as the heavens are higher than the earth, so are My ways higher than your ways, and My thoughts than your thoughts." – Isaiah 55:8-9

- Our trust in God Almighty should not wane in times of great difficulties and challenges. God is with you and His word to you will not go waste. He said "for as the rain comes down, and the snow from heaven, and do not return there, but water the earth, and make it bring forth and bud, that it may give seed to the sower and bread to the eater. So shall My word be that goes forth from My mouth. It shall not return to Me void, but it shall accomplish what I please, and it shall prosper in the thing for which I sent it."-Isaiah 55:10-11.
- We saw in Joseph's case that it was God's plan to save people from the coming famine. Joseph and his brothers did not know anything about that. God sent forth his word to save people and Joseph was part of His plan.
- God's plan always involves the salvation and well being of people.

Conclusion

We studied that Joseph's great grandfather Abraham obeyed the voice of God as a former idol worshipper. Through this obedience, you change allegiance to who you worship. Abraham chose to worship God Almighty. This is the first step in becoming a child of God.

Humanity was created in God's image to have an everlasting intimate loving relationship with the Creator. "Then God said, "Let us make man in Our image, according to Our likeness, let them have dominion over the fish of the sea, over the birds of the air, ad over the cattle, over all the earth and over every creeping thing that creeps on the earth."-Gen 1:26

This was a great plan for humanity. However, mankind lost this relationship through deception from the devil and evil one, Satan. The devil managed to use trickery in luring the first man and woman to disbelieve God's perfect word for them. They acted on the lies of Satan and lost that great relationship and total dependent on God Almighty. God's love did not fade away after the decision to live independent of Him. The price of this spiritual crisis was the ushering in of 'sin and death.' Creation then went into a state of declining and dying. The only way this price was to be paid was for another person free from the line of Adam to die to save all humanity.

God so loved us that He chose to die for us to restore that lost relationship between us. It was a painful death as He took on humanity and experienced all the temptation and pain we go through. This makes Him a better person to understand our plight.

Before the coming of Jesus Christ to pay for the price once and for all, God established other temporal measures. One of the prominent ones was the yearly killing of animals to atone for the sins of the children of God. God has been reaching to humanity right from the time of Adam and Eves' disobedience. He has been communicating through prophets of old and finally through His Son Jesus Christ. This is where we start.

"In the past God spoke to our forefathers through the prophets at many times and in various ways, but in these days He has spoken to us by His Son, whom he appointed heir of all things, and through whom He made the universe."-Hebrew 1:1

The invitation to receive the gift is open to all.
God loves us so much so that He died to pay for our sin. "For God so loved the world that He gave His only begotten Son, that whosoever believes in Him should have everlasting life. -John 3:16. God sent Jesus to come and save us from our sin and to forgive us. 'For God did not send His Son into the world to condemn the world, but that the world through Him might be saved."-Verse17. Anyone who believe and accept Jesus Christ's gift of eternal life will not be condemned. "He who believes in Him (Jesus Christ) is not condemned, but he who does not

believe is condemned already because he has not believed in the name of the Son of God." Vs. 18

We need to open the door of our heart (spiritual life) and invite Jesus Christ into it for a loving intimate relationship. "Behold, I stand at the door and knock, if anyone hears My voice and opens the door, I will come in to him and dine with him, and he with Me."-Rev 3:20

Our response should be the same as the people who asked the apostle Peter what they should do. After preaching the good news to the people they asked him what to do. This is what is needed to be done: "repent and let every one of you be baptised in the name of Jesus Christ for the remission of sins and you shall receive the gift of the Holy Spirit." Acts 2:38

Accept the free gift by faith and the personal forgiveness of sin Jesus Christ offers to you. This will ensure your total victory forever, to accept the finished work of Jesus Christ on the cross. "...The gift of God is eternal life in Christ Jesus."-Rom 6:23b

Once we repent of our sins and confess Jesus as our Lord and Saviour, we now become part of the family of God. The good news is that although there may exist a curse along our family lines due to idol worship, we become part of this new family without any curse. Jesus Christ became a curse for us. The apostle Paul's said, "therefore, if anyone is in Christ, he is a new creation, old things have passed away, behold all things have become new."-2Cor 5:17

There is a scripture verse that I was given on the day I accepted and trusted the Lord Jesus Christ as my Saviour: " But as many as received Him, to them He gave the right to become the children of God, to those who believe in His name."- John 1:12

I pray you also become one of God's children. Amen